CORNISH GR
BEGIN
AND THE AUXILIARY VERBS

by JOHN PAGE

Bard of the Cornish Gorsedd

An lyver ma yw profys
yn uvel dhe Gernow.
Re vywo hy yeth bys vynitha

Kesva an Taves Kernewek, mis Metheven 2002

Fifth (revised) edition, October 1993
reprinted January 1996
Sixth (revised) edition, June 2002

Kesva an Taves Kernewek

(The Cornish Language Board)

ISBN 1 902917 26 X

RAGLAVAR

The first edition of this book was published privately by the author in 1977, and the second edition by Kowethas an Yeth Kernewek in 1981. The author's preface to the third edition (Kowethas an Yeth Kernewek, 1982) says:

'This book contains all the grammar that is required for the Elementary Grade of the Cornish Language Board's examinations, and it contains nothing beyond that level. The paragraph headings are those of the Board's own syllabus.

'Some of the material in the section on auxiliary verbs will be required for Grade 1, notably the third person singular of the present and past tenses, and the remainder will be required for Grade 2.

'There is also an Appendix on the system of mutation.'

Dr Ken George edited the fourth edition. Editor's preface to the fourth edition (1988):

'John Page, the author of this work, was an interpreter by profession, and a grammarian of the old school. Upon retirement, he added Cornish to his impressive list of languages, and having passed all three grades in one year, began to teach it in Truro. He was for a time the General Secretary of the Cornish Language Board. Although he left Cornwall for some years to travel on the continent, he returned, and ran an active class in Luxulyan up to the time of his death in 1984.

'It is as a tribute to John Page's expertise in logical presentation that this little book has been chosen as the first Cornish text-book to be re-written using the revised spelling. The editor hopes that he would have approved of this major change. It is also the first text-book to be produced on a word processor. The text has been edited and slightly revised. References to page numbers in P.A.S. Pool's Cornish for Beginners *have been omitted.'*

Preface to the sixth edition

The adoption of Kernewek Kemmyn by the Cornish Language Board and the publication by the Board of the second edition of *A Grammar of Modern Cornish* by Wella Brown and the *Gerlyver Kernewek Kemmyn* by Dr Ken George have necessitated some minor changes to John Page's well-tested work.

CONTENTS

CORNISH GRAMMAR FOR BEGINNERS

THE AUXILIARY VERBS

CORNISH GRAMMAR FOR BEGINNERS

I NOUNS

Nouns are either masculine or feminine, there being no neuter gender. Gender follows sex in the case of animate beings, but there are few guidelines for the gender of inanimate objects. All nouns of more than one syllable ending in **-enn** are feminine. Gender must be learned by heart.

There are also few guidelines for plural forms, although many end in **-ow** or **-yow**. Nouns borrowed from English form plurals with **-s** or **-ys**, though there is a tendency nowadays to replace the latter with **-ow**.

dowr	**dowrow**	*water*	*waters*
chi	**chiow**	*house*	*houses*
gorhel	**gorholyon**	*ship*	*ships*
klas	**klasys, klasow**	*class*	*classes*

Some words undergo internal change (cf. English *foot, feet; man, men*)

yar	**yer**	*chicken*	*chickens*
margh	**mergh**	*horse*	*horses*
lowarn	**lewern**	*fox*	*foxes*
edhen	**ydhyn**	*bird*	*birds*
tiek	**tiogyon**	*farmer*	*farmers*

The gender and plural should be learned when the word itself is learned.

II   THE DEFINITE ARTICLE

The definite article *'the'* in Cornish is **an**. It mutates feminine singular nouns and masculine plural nouns of <u>persons</u> to State 2 (see Appendix 1). Feminine plurals and masculine plural of <u>things</u> are not mutated:

mamm	**an vamm**	*mother*	*the mother*
krows	**an grows**	*cross*	*the cross*
gwydhenn	**an wydhenn**	*tree*	*the tree*
an tiek	**an diogyon**	*the farmer*	*the farmers*
an pons	**an ponsow**	*the bridge*	*the bridges*

There are a few exceptions and strange mutations, notably:

mergh	**an vergh**	*horses*	*the horses*
meyn	**an veyn**	*stones*	*the stones*
dydh	**an jydh**	*day*	*the day*
dew	**an dhew**	*two* (m)	*the two*
diw	**an dhiw**	*two* (f)	*the two*
dor	**an nor**	*ground*	*the world*

III   ADJECTIVES

In Cornish, adjectives normally follow the noun, although there are a few exceptions, notably **hen** *'old'* and **tebel** *'evil'*. When an adjective precedes a noun it will mutate it to State 2:

chi bras	*a big house*
an den koth	*the old man*
an hen borth	*the ancient harbour*
an debel venyn	*the evil woman*

A feminine singular noun and a masculine plural of persons mutate their adjective even when they themselves are not mutated:

benyn deg	*a pretty woman*
an venyn deg	*the pretty woman*
tiogyon dha	*good farmers*
an diogyon dha	*the good farmers*

Adjectives take over the demonstrative from the noun:

an chi ma	*this house*
an chi koth ma	*this old house*

If there are more than one adjective, the last accepts the demonstrative:

an chi koth bras ma	*this big old house*

When there is more than one adjective, only the first will be mutated (where mutation occurs):

an wydhenn goth bras ma	*this big old tree*

Adjectives do not form plurals:

an chi koth	*the old house*
an chiow koth	*the old houses*

Nouns ending in **-s** and **-th**, even if feminine, do not mutate their adjectives when these begin with **k-**, **p-**, **t-**:

an eglos teg	*the fine church*
an gath plos	*the dirty cat*

IV   POSSESSION

Possession is expressed in Cornish by putting first the thing possessed followed by the possessor:

ki an tiek   *the farmer's dog*
chi ow mamm   *my mother's house*

Note that the definite article or the possessive appears (as indeed in English) before the possessor and not the possessed.

If the possessor is indefinite, no article appears:

ki tiek   *a farmer's dog*
keun tiogyon   *farmers' dogs*

The same rule applies in remoter possessive situations:

chi mab an tiek   *the farmer's son's house*

It will be seen that the word order is the reverse of English and that the definite article appears only once.

V   PRONOUNS: PERSONAL, POSSESSIVE, SUFFIXED

Personal		Possessive		Suffixed	
my	*I*	**ow**[3]	*my*	**vy**	**ma**
ty	*you* (s)	**dha**[2]	*your* (s)	**jy**	**ta**
ev	*he*	**y**[2]	*his*	**ev**	**va**
hi	*she*	**hy**[3]	*her*	**hi**	
ni	*we*	**agan**	*our*	**ni**	
hwi	*you* (p)	**agas**	*your* (p)	**hwi**	
i	*they*	**aga**[3]	*their*	**i**	

Note that **agan** *'our'* and **agas** *'your'* are the only two possessives that do not cause mutation (see Appendix 1):

ow thas	*my father*
dha das	*your father*
y das	*his father*
hy thas	*her father*
agan tas	*our father*
agas tas	*your father*
aga thas	*their father*

The suffixed or 'enclitic' pronouns are used for emphasis or to avoid confusion, but are otherwise optional:

ow thas vy yw hir	*my father is tall*
mes dha das jy yw berr	*but* **your** *father is short*

The suffixed enclitics in the first column are often stressed, and written as separate words; those in the second column (i.e. **ma, ta, va**) are unstressed, and joined to the preceding word. Note that there is a difference in spelling and pronunciation between **hi** *'she'* and **hy** *'her'*:

hi a wel hy hath hi	*she sees her cat*

In affirmative statements (only), all of the personal pronouns are used with the 3rd person singular of the verb:

my yw skwith	*I am tired*
i a vynn gweles an	*they want to see the*
chi nowydh	*new house*

This, however, applies only when the pronoun precedes the verb, as we shall see later.

VI   THE PRESENT PARTICIPLE

The present participle (English *'-ing'*) is formed by placing in front of the infinitive or 'dictionary' form of the verb, the particle **ow**[4] before consonants or **owth** before vowels or an initial **h**:

kana	*to sing*	**ow kana**	*singing*
gwari	*to play*	**ow kwari**	*playing*
eva	*to drink*	**owth eva**	*drinking*

One must be careful to distinguish between a true participle and a verbal noun:

yma tas ow redya	*father is reading*	(participle)
tas a gar redya	*father likes reading*	(verbal noun)

The 'long' form of **bos** *'to be'* must be used with the present participle:

yma an tiek ow konis y has
the farmer is sowing his seed

yth esov vy ow tos
I am coming

nyns usi Yowann owth eva y gorev
John is not drinking his beer

ha(g) *'and'* when used with the present participle gives the meaning *'when'*, *'while'*:

hag ev ow redya
when (while) he was reading

ha my ow mos dhe Borthia
as I was going to St Ives

This usage appears to advantage in sentences otherwise requiring the present participle of **bos** *'to be'*, which can then be omitted:

ev a brenas lyver hag ev yn Truru
he bought a book when he was in Truro

ha hi yn Truru, hi a welas Yowann
being in Truro, she saw John

VII   THE PRESENT TENSE OF 'BOS', 'GWELES', 'MYNNES', 'GALLOES'

(1)   **bos** *'to be'*

short form	long form	
ov (vy)	**esov (vy)**	*I am*
os (jy)	**esos (jy)**	*you* (s) *are*
yw (ev)	**yma* (ev)**	*he/it is*
yw (hi)	**yma* (hi)**	*she/it is*
on (ni)	**eson (ni)**	*we are*
owgh (hwi)	**esowgh (hwi)**	*you* (p) *are*
yns (i)	**ymons* (i)**	*they are*

*in the interrogative and negative **yma** is replaced by **eus** or **usi**, and **ymons** by **esons**.

The short form is used when the complement of the verb is descriptive of the subject, i.e. a noun or adjective:

den koth ov vy	*I am an old man*
skwith yns i	*they are tired*

The long form is used when the complement locates the subject or tells us what it is doing:

yma Yowann y'n chi	*John is in the house*
ymons i ow koska	*they are sleeping*

11

(2)   **gweles** *'to see'*

This is an example of a reasonably regular verb without vowel affection. The infinitive consists of two parts, the stem **gwel-** and the ending **-es**. Other endings indicate the tense and person. The present tense is:

gwel*av*	*I see*
gwel*ydh*	*you* (s) *see*
gwel	*he/she/it sees*
gwel*yn*	*we see*
gwel*owgh*	*you* (p) *see*
gwel*ons*	*they see*

The mutations undergone by **gweles** are:

State 2:	particles **a, na, ny, re**	**GW**	**>**	**W**
State 4:	particle **ow**	**GW**	**>**	**KW**
State 5:	particle **y**	**GW**	**>**	**HW**

In a simple affirmative sentence, when the subject precedes the verb, this will remain in the 3rd person singular, and the particle will be **a²**:

my a wel an chi	*I see the house*
i a wel an mor	*they see the sea*

When the object precedes the verb, this must be made to agree with its subject:

an chi a welav vy	*I see the house*
an mor a welons i	*they see the sea*

When an adverb (or anything else except the subject) starts the sentence, the particle will be **y⁵** and the verb made to agree with its subject:

omma y hwelav an chi	*here I see the house*
ena y hwelons i an mor	*there they see the sea*

Which of these forms is used depends upon the emphasis to be conveyed, the principle being that whatever comes first in the sentence receives the emphasis. Thus **my a wel an chi** implies that *I* see the house (perhaps you don't), while **an chi a welav vy** implies that it is the *house* that I see (and not the church). The third form is for use with a preceding adverb or adverbial phrase.

(3) **gul** *'to do'*   **mynnes** *'to want'*   **galloes** *'to be able'*

See the section on Auxiliary Verbs, where the full conjugation and guidance for usage is to be found.

VIII   THE PRESENT TENSE OF 'KARA', 'MOS', 'DOS'

Beginners are required to know only the 3rd person singular (i.e. the form for *'he'*, *'she'*, *'it'* and noun subjects).

(1) **kara** *'to like, love'*

As is usual with most Cornish regular verbs, the 3rd person singular is the bare stem of the verb (cf. **gwel-** from **gweles**, VII 2)

The form for **kara** is therefore **kar** *'he/she loves'*.

The only mutation undergone is State 2 **K > G**, since State 4 and 5 do not affect the letter **K** (see Appendix 1). We therefore write:

Yowann a gar y vroder   *John loves his brother*
or   (adverb) + **y kar Yowann y vroder**

The third choice, that of putting the object first, is ambiguous, since:

y vroder a gar Yowann

could easily be read as *'his brother loves John'*.

Two further examples:

hi a gar hy hath
she loves her cat
an fleghes a gar aga mamm
the children love their mother

Note that although the noun *'children'* is plural the verb remains in the singular. This is always the case when the subject precedes the verb.

(2)   **mos**   *'to go'*

mos is a very irregular verb and does not follow the usual pattern. The 3rd person singular of the present tense is simply:

     a   *he, she, it goes*

It does not accept the **a** particle, and before the vowel the **y** particle becomes **yth**:

an tren ma a dhe Bennsans
this train goes to Penzance

dhe Loundres yth a an tren na
that train goes to London

(3)   **dos**   *'to come'*

dos is another irregular verb and its 3rd person singular tense is:

     deu   *he, she, it comes*

Unlike **mos**, this does accept the **a** particle and the mutations undergone are:

State 2	**a** particle	**D** >	**DH**
State 4	**ow** particle	**D** >	**T**
State 5	**y** particle	**D** >	**T**

We have therefore:

mamm a dheu hedhyw   *mother comes today*
hedhyw y teu mamm

gwav a dheu   *winter comes*
yma gwav ow tos   *winter is coming*

(4) **gul**   *'to do'*,   **mynnes** *'to want'*,   **galloes** *'to be able'*

For these verbs see the section on Auxiliary Verbs, where the full conjugation and examples of usage are given.

IX 'MEDHES' IN DIALOGUE

This verb is used for reporting direct speech as follows:

yn-medhav *I said*   **yn-medhyn** *we said*
yn-medhydh *you* (s) *said*   **yn-medhowgh** *you* (p) *said*
yn-medh ev *he said*   **yn-medhons** *they said*
yn-medh hi *she said*

Note that previous textbooks gave only the 1st singular and plural forms, because only these were recorded in the traditional texts.

'Teg yw Morwenna,' yn-medh ev
'Morwenna is pretty,' he said

'Ny allav,' yn-medh Yowann
'I can't,' said John

'Da yw henna,' yn-medhons i
'That's good,' they said

The verb **medhes** cannot be used for reporting indirect speech; i.e. *'he said that ...'* is translated by **ev a leveris ...**

15

X   QUESTIONS

The interrogative particle is **a²**, and the negative interrogative is **a ny²**:

a gar an tiek y gi ?	*does the farmer love his dog ?*
a yll Yowann dos ?	*can John come ?*
a ny vynn ev dybri ?	*doesn't he want to eat ?*

However, the particle is not used with those tenses of **bos** and **mos** that begin with a vowel:

yw henna gwir ?	*is that true ?*
a y das ev ?	*is his father going ?*

In negative questions with these tenses **ny** becomes **nyns**:

a nyns yw henna gwir ?	*isn't that true ?*
a nyns a Yowann ?	*isn't John going ?*

There are also words that ask questions:

(1) **py ?**   *'what ?'*,   *'which ?'* is used adjectivally with nouns:

py lyver yw henna ?	*which book is that ?*
py den a dheu hedhyw ?	*what man is coming today ?*

(2) **pyth ?** *'what'* is used pronominally when there is no noun:

pyth yw hemma ?	*what is this ?*

When position is involved in such actions as this, the long form of **bos** must be used; and **yma** and **ymons** will become **eus** or **usi** and **esons** respectively:

py den eus y'n chi ?	*which man is in the house ?*
pyth eus war an voes ?	*what is on the table ?*

This will also apply when the question is about an action:

pyth usi hi ow kana ?	*what is she singing ?*

(3) **pandra ?**   *'what ?'* is used with verbs:

pandr'a gar ev ?	*what does he like ?*
pandr'a vynnons ?	*what do they want ?*

(4) **piw ?** *'who ?'* will require the long or short form of **bos** depending on whether position or action are involved or not:

piw yw henna ?	*who is that ?*
piw eus y'n chi ?	*who is in the house ?*

(5) **ple ?** (**ple'th ?** before vowels) *'where ?'* necessarily involves position, so the long form of **bos** must be used. It is a contraction of **py le ?** *'what place ?'*, and it combines with **yma** to form **ple'ma ?** *'where is he, she, it ?'* and with **ymons** to form **ple'mons ?** *'where are they ?'*:

ple'ma dha gi ?	*where is your dog ?*
ple'mons i hedhyw ?	*where are they today ?*

ple ? mutates the b-tenses of **bos** to State 5: **B** > **F**:

ple fydh hi hedhyw ?	*where will she be today ?*
ple fydhons i ?	*where will they be ?*

XI REPLIES TO QUESTIONS

Affirmative replies are made by repeating the operative verb in the radical or unmutated form in the appropriate person, tense and number, but without enclitics:

yw Morwenna lowen ?	**yw**
is Morwenna happy ?	*yes*
usi Yowann y'n chi ?	**usi**
is John in the house ?	*yes*
a vynnons i dos ? .	**mynnons**
do they want to come ?	*yes*

Negative replies prefix **na²**, or **nag** before vowels in **bos** and **mos**:

yw Morwenna lowen ?	**nag yw**
usi Yowann y'n chi ?	**nag usi**
a vynnons i dos ?	**na vynnons**

This usage tends to be clumsy when conjugating verbs, so there is a tendency in speech to substitute the appropriate form of the auxiliary verb **gul**:

a garas ev an vowes ?	**gwrug**
did he like the girl	*yes*

In rapid colloquial speech it is difficult to resist a tendency to introduce words for *'yes'* and *'no'*; Late Cornish usage suggests for these **ya** ['I.a] and **na** ['na:].

XII SECOND PERSON IMPERATIVES

The imperative is the 'command' form of the verb - *'do this'*, *'don't do that'*, *'drink your tea'*, etc.

The singular form is nearly always the bare stem of the verb:

red dha lyver !	*read your book !*
mir orth henna !	*look at that !*

In the plural, most verbs add **-ewgh** to the stem; verbs in **-ya** add **-yewgh**:

redyewgh agas lyver !	*read your books !*
mirewgh orth henna !	*look at that !*

For the negative, prefix **na²**:

na red an lyver na !	*don't read that book !*
na vir orth Yowann !	*don't look at John !*

There are some notable irregularities:

ke ! *go !* **deus !** *come !* **ro !** *give !* **bydh !** *be !*

In the plural, these four become:

kewgh ! dewgh ! rewgh ! bedhewgh

It is always possible to form an imperative by using the auxiliary verb **gul** (see the section on Auxiliary Verbs)):

gwra igeri an daras !   *open the door !*
na wrewgh poenya !   *do not run !*

With an unfamiliar verb this may be the best way out of a difficulty. In the 'direct' form, the two above examples would read:

igor an daras !   **na boenyewgh !**

To soften the command, imperatives are usually followed by **mar pleg** *'if you please':*

deus omma, mar pleg   *come here, please*

XIII CARDINAL AND ORDINAL NUMBERS

Cardinal 0-20: **mann, onan (unn), dew (diw), tri (teyr), peswar (peder), pymp, hwegh, seyth, eth, naw, deg, unnek, dewdhek, trydhek, peswardhek, pymthek, hwetek, seytek, etek, nownsek, ugens.**

Ordinal 1st-20th: **kynsa, nessa, tressa, peswara, pympes, hweghves, seythves, ethves, nawves, degves, unnegves, dewdhegves, trydhegves, peswardhegves, pymthegves, hwetegves, seytegves, etegves, nownsegves, ugensves.**

Beyond 20 there are no new terms for the numbers except **hanter-kans** *'50',* **kans** (m) *'100'* and **mil** (m) *'1000'*.

1 is **onan** when used alone and for counting, but **unn** when used as an adjective. It mutates a feminine singular noun to State 2:

unn den   *one man*   **unn venyn**   *one woman*

19

2 has the masculine form **dew** and the feminine form **diw**. They both mutate their nouns to State 2 and are themselves mutated by the definite article:

dew dhen	*two men*	**an dhew dhen**	*the two men*
diw venyn	*two women*	**an dhiw venyn**	*the two women*

3 has the masculine form **tri** and the feminine form **teyr**. They both mutate their nouns to State 3 but are not mutated by the definite article:

(an) tri hi	*the) three dogs*
(an) teyr hath	*(the) three cats*

The form **trysa** is to be regarded as the truer form of the ordinal *'third'*; **tressa** is formed analogously from **nessa**.

4 has the masculine form **peswar** and the feminine form **peder**. Neither causes mutation:

peswar ki	*four dogs*
peder kath	*four cats*

From 5 onwards there are no feminine forms (except in such expressions as **teyr bugh warn ugens** *'twenty-three cows'*). Note that the thing enumerated stays in the singular.

After 20 we begin all over again:

21	**onan war ugens**
22	**dew warn ugens** etc. until
29	**naw warn ugens**

30 has no separate word but is expressed as:

30	**deg warn ugens**
31	**unnek warn ugens** etc.

40 is expressed as **dew-ugens** *'two score'*. We then go on reckoning in scores, using the coupling word **ha** *'and'*:

41 **onan ha dew-ugens**
42 **dew ha dew-ugens**
49 **naw ha dew-ugens**

Then comes 50, which is either **deg ha dew-ugens** or, more usually, **hanter-kans** *'half a hundred'*.

60 is **triugens** *'three twenties'*, 70 is **deg ha triugens**, 80 is **peswar ugens** *'four twenties'* (cf. French *quatre-vingts*), and 90 **deg ha peswar ugens**. 100 is **kans**, and one can use this in numbers between 100 and 199 inclusive:

168 **kans eth ha triugens**

It is more traditional, however, to continue reckoning in scores up to 200:

168 **eth hag eth ugens**

In compound numbers the thing enumerated remains in the singular and is placed between the two parts of the number:

pymp den warn ugens   *25 men*
deg lyver warn ugens   *30 books*

This also applies to ordinals:

hy fympes penn-bloedh ha dew-ugens
her 45th birthday

Note that the second part of the number remains in the cardinal form. **nessa** *'second'* also has the meaning *'next'*:

ev a drig y'n nessa chi   *he lives in the next house*

Finally, note that ordinal numbers used as adjectives precede their nouns:

an tressa dydh	*the third day*
an degves den	*the tenth man*

XIV   INFINITIVES

The infinitive is the 'name' or 'dictionary' form of the verb and it is the form used with the auxiliaries **gul**, **galloes** and **mynnes** (q.v.):

my a wra mos	*I shall go*
ev a yll gweles	*he can see*
ni a vynn dybri	*we want to eat*

It is also used as a verbal noun:

ev a gar redya	*he likes reading*
y gana yw teg	*his singing is fine*
gweles yw krysi	*seeing is believing*
kales yw dyski	*learning is difficult*

An important use of the infinitive is with the possessives, when a pronoun is the object of the sentence:

my a vynn y weles	*I want to see him (I want his seeing)*
ev a yll hy klywes	*he can hear her*

For emphasis the enclitics may be used:

my a vynn y weles ev   **ev a yll hy klywes hi**

Note that the infinitive will mutate to the requirements of the possessive; see V. For further details of this usage, see the section on Auxiliary Verbs.

XV   THE IMPERFECT TENSE OF 'BOS'

The 3rd person singular of this tense is:

short form	**o**
long form	**esa**

As we have seen, the **a** particle is not used with those tenses of **bos** beginning with a vowel. The **y** particle is replaced by **yth**, and used when the verb starts the phrase. The short form is used for descriptive complements, and the long form for location or action:

an den o hir	*the man was tall*
hir o an den	
yth esa ev y'n dre	*he was in the town*
yth esa hi ow kana	*she was singing*

Questions are asked simply by putting the verb first, since there is no **a** particle:

o hir dha das jy ?	*was your father tall ?*
esa hi y'n eglos ?	*was she in the church ?*

The negative particle is **nyns** and negative questions are asked with **a nyns**:

nyns o toemm an dowr	*the water was not warm*
a nyns o toemm an dowr ?	*wasn't the water warm ?*

XVI   THE PRETERITE TENSE OF 'GWELES'

The preterite tense deals with an action completed in the past, cf. English *sell, I sold; see, I saw.*

In Cornish, the preterite tense is formed by adding the following endings to the stem of the verb:

-is   -sys   -as (or **-is**)   **-syn   -sowgh   -sons**

gwelis	*I saw*
gwelsys	*you* (s) *saw*
gwelas	*he, she, it saw*
gwelsyn	*we saw*
gwelsowgh	*you* (p) *saw*
gwelsons	*they saw*

Those verbs that have -is as the ending of the 3rd person singular include:

- all verbs ending in **-el (kewsel, ev a gewsis)**

- many (but not all) verbs ending in **-i**, e.g.

dybri	*to eat*	**prederi**	*to think*
gorthybi	*to answer*	**synsi**	*to hold*
krysi	*to believe*	**tevi**	*to grow*
pysi	*to pray*	**tybi**	*to think*

ev a welas an ki	*he saw the dog*
ni a dhybris an bara	*we ate the bread*

XVII PRETERITE TENSE OF 'KARA', 'MOS', 'DOS'

At first Cornish speakers only need to know the 3rd person singular of these verbs.

1) **kara** follows the 'regular' rule of **gweles**, and the 3rd person singular of the preterite tense is **karas**:

ev a garas y das	*he loved his father*
prest y karas hi hy hath	*she loved her cat always*

2) **mos** is very irregular, and the 3rd person singular is **eth**. This does not accept the **a** particle, and the **y** particle is replaced by **yth**:

an tiek eth tre	*the farmer went home*
yn skon yth eth an den	*the man went quickly*

3) **dos** is also irregular, and the 3rd person singular is **deuth**. This does accept the **a** particle and mutates to State 2:

ev a dheuth de	*he came yesterday*
myttin y teuth dew dhen	*in the morning two men came*

The negative forms will be:

nyns eth ev	*he did not go*
ny dheuth ev	*he did not come*

and the interrogative:

eth ev ?	*did he go ?*
a dheuth ev ?	*did he come ?*

and, finally, the negative interrogative:

a nyns eth ev ?	*didn't he go ?*
a ny dheuth ev ?	*didn't he come ?*

XVIII   THE PERFECTIVE PARTICLE 'RE'

The particle **re²** gives 'perfect' meaning to the preterite tense, i.e. '*I have seen*' in place of '*I saw*':

ev a welas y vroder	*he saw his brother*
ev re welas y vroder	*he has seen his brother*

Before vowels in **mos** the particle becomes **res**:

an medhyk eth	*the doctor went*
an medhyk res eth	*the doctor has gone*

re does not mutate the b-tenses of **bos**.

re cannot be used interrogatively or negatively, and in such cases the precise meaning must be derived from the context:

eth an medhyk ?	*has the doctor gone ?*
nag eth, yma ev y'n chi	*no, he's in the house*

PRONOMIAL PREPOSITIONS

gans	*(with)*	**dhe**	*(to)*
genev	*with me*	**dhymm**	*to me*
genes	*with you* (s)	**dhis**	*to you* (s)
ganso	*with him/it*	**dhodho**	*to him/it*
gensi	*with her/it*	**dhedhi**	*to her/it*
genen	*with us*	**dhyn**	*to us*
genowgh	*with you* (p)	**dhywgh**	*to you* (p)
gansa	*with them*	**dhedha**	*to them*
war	*(on)*	**heb**	*(without)*
warnav	*on me*	**hebov**	*without me*
warnas	*on you* (s)	**hebos**	*without you* (s)
warnodho	*on him/it*	**hebdho**	*without him/it*
warnedhi	*on her/it*	**hebdhi**	*without her/it*
warnan	*on us*	**hebon**	*without us*
warnowgh	*on you* (p)	**hebowgh**	*without you* (p)
warnedha	*on them*	**hebdha**	*without them*
rag	*(for)*	**yn**	*(in)*
ragov	*for me*	**ynnov**	*in me*
ragos	*for you* (s)	**ynnos**	*in you* (s)
ragdho	*for him/it*	**ynno**	*in him/it*
rygdhi	*for her/it*	**ynni**	*in her/it*
ragon	*for us*	**ynnon**	*in us*
ragowgh	*for you* (p)	**ynnowgh**	*in you* (p)
ragdha	*for them*	**ynna**	*in them*

orth	(at)	a	(from)
orthiv	at me	ahanav	from me
orthis	at you (s)	ahanas	from you (p)
orto	at him/it	anodho	from him/it
orti	at her/it	anedhi	from her/it
orthyn	at us	ahanan	from us
orthowgh	at you (p)	ahanowgh	from you
orta	at them	anedha	from them

The enclitics are often added for emphasis:

chi ha den ynno ev	a house with a man in it
ev eth hebdhi hi	he went without her

With its enclitic, **dhymm** becomes **dhymmo vy** and **dhis** becomes **dhiso jy**:

ev a dheuth dhymmo vy	he came to me
hi eth dhiso jy	she went to you

XX   IDIOMS WITH 'GANS' AND 'DHE'

yma gans means 'to have' in the sense of 'having on one, with one' and **yma dhe** means 'to have' in the sense of owning, possessing.

yma genev ki	I have a dog (here with me)
yma ki dhymm	I own a dog
eus pluvenn genes ?	have you got a pen (on you) ?
nyns eus gwreg dhymm	I haven't got a wife

In the past tense, **yth esa**, **esa** and **nyns esa** are used:

yth esa ki dhymm	I had a dog
esa ki dhodho ?	did he have a dog ?
nyns esa pluvenn ganso	he had no pen (with him)

28

This idiom is also used with emotions, needs and desires:

yma nown dhymm	*I'm hungry*
eus syghes dhis ?	*are you thirsty ?*
yma edhomm dhyn a vara	*we need bread*
yth esa own dhedhi	*she was afraid*

but note that *'glad'* and *'sorry'* require the short form of **bos**:

da yw genev dha weles	*I'm glad to see you*
drog o gensi	*she was sorry*

XXI   DEMONSTRATIVE PRONOUNS AND ADJECTIVES

hemma	**ma**	*this* (m)
henna	**na**	*that* (m)
homma	**ma**	*this* (f)
honna	**na**	*that* (f)

Before **yw** and **o** these contract to **hemm, henn, homm, honn**.

henn yw an gwiryonedh	*that is the truth*
henn o teg	*that was fine*
piw yw homma ?	*who is this* (f) *?*
pyth yw henna ?	*what is that ?*

The forms **ma** and **na** follow the noun enclitically when used as adjectival particles:

an chi ma	*this house*
an gath na	*that cat*

When the noun is qualified by an adjective, the demonstrative follows the adjective (see also III):

an chi bras na	*that big house*
an gath wynn ma	*this white cat*

'*These*' and '*those*' as pronouns are: **an re ma, an re na**:

an re ma yw da	*these are good*
an re na yw drog	*those are bad*

'*Some ...others*'   is   **re ... re erell**:

re yw da, re erell yw drog	*some are good, others are bad*

XXII   NEGATIVE SENTENCES

The phrase starts with the negative particle, which is **nyns** before vowels in **bos** and **mos,** and **ny^2** otherwise:

ny gar an den ma korev	*this man doesn't like beer*
nyns yw mamm lowen	*mother isn't happy*
nyns ov vy lowen	*I am not happy*
nyns eth ev tre	*he didn't go home*
ny welsons i an chi	*they didn't see the house*

Note that it is possible, but less common, to begin the phrase with the subject, but that if this is a plural noun, the verb must also be plural:

mebyon vras ny wrons oela
big boys don't cry

As a negative reply, i.e. a plain '*no*', **ny** becomes **nag** before vowels in **bos** and **mos**, otherwise **na^2**:

os ta lowen ? nag ov	*are you happy ? no*
esons i omma ? nag esons	*are they here ? no*

Here are some examples using verbs other than **bos**:

ny wel an vowes an mor	*the girl does not see the sea*
ny welav an mor	*I don't see the sea*
a welowgh hwi an mor ?	*do you see the sea ?*
na welyn	*no*
ny welyn an mor	*we don't see the sea*

30

gwenton	*spring*	**kynyav**	*autumn*
hav	*summer*	**gwav**	*winter*

yn hav yth yw toemm an howl *in summer the sun is warm*
yn gwav yth yw noeth an gwydh *in winter the trees are bare*
gwenton a dheu yn skon *spring is coming soon*

mis Genver	*January*	**mis Gortheren**	*July*
mis Hwevrer	*February*	**mis Est**	*August*
mis Meurth	*March*	**mis Gwynngala**	*September*
mis Ebryl	*April*	**mis Hedra**	*October*
mis Me	*May*	**mis Du**	*November*
mis Metheven	*June*	**mis Kevardhu**	*December*

dy' Sul	*Sunday*	**Nadelik**	*Christmas*
dy' Lun	*Monday*	**Stoel**	*Epiphany*
dy' Meurth	*Tuesday*	**Pask**	*Easter*
dy' Mergher	*Wednesday*	**Penkast**	*Pentecost*
dy' Yow	*Thursday*	**Goelowann**	*Midsummer*
dy' Gwener	*Friday*	**Goeldheys**	*Harvest*
dy' Sadorn	*Saturday*	**Dy'goel Pyran**	*Piran's Day*

Nadelik yw an 25ens mis Kevardhu
Christmas is the 25th of December
kynsa mis Me yw dy'goel
the first of May is a holiday
Goelowann a vydh dy' Yow hevlyna
Midsummer will be a Thursday this year
ow fenn-bloedh yw an 19ves mis Hedra
my birthday is the 19th of October
py dydh yw hedhyw ? Dy' Lun an degves mis Me yw
what day is it today ? It's Monday the 10th of May

py eur yw ?   *what is the time ?*

0600	**hwegh eur**
0605	**pymp mynysenn wosa hwegh**
0615	**kwarter wosa hwegh**
0630	**hwegh eur ha hanter**
0645	**kwarter dhe seyth**
0655	**pymp mynysenn dhe seyth**
0659	**ogas dhe** *(nearly)* **seyth**
0700	**seyth eur poran** *(exactly)*
1200	**hanter-dydh**
2400	**hanter-nos**

myttin	*morning*	**gorthugher**	*evening*
dohajydh	*afternoon*	**nos**	*night*

nos dha dhywgh hwi ! *good night to you !*

When you have mastered all the above points of grammar, you have sufficient grounding in the language to tackle the First Grade examination, and you can pass on to the second volume in this series, *Grammar Beyond the First Grade,* which contains the grammar required for higher grades.

Gwas Kenedhlow

THE AUXILIARY VERBS

The auxiliary verbs are three in number and are so called because they help other verbs to have further meanings.

The verb **gul** means 'to do' when used as an auxiliary, and 'to make' when used as a verb in its own right. The verb **mynnes** means 'to wish' or 'to want', and the verb **galloes** means 'to be able'.

1) THE CONJUGATION AND USE OF 'GUL'

present tense		imperfect tense	
gwrav	*I do*	**gwren**	*I was doing*
gwredh	*you* (s) *do*	**gwres**	*you* (s) *were doing*
gwra	*he, she does*	**gwre**	*he, she was doing*
gwren	*we do*	**gwren**	*we were doing*
gwrewgh	*you* (p) *do*	**gwrewgh**	*you* (p) *were doing*
gwrons	*they do*	**gwrens**	*they were doing*

preterite tense		conditional tense	
gwrug	*I did*	**gwrussen**	*I would do*
gwrussys	*you* (s) *did*	**gwrusses**	*you* (s) *would do*
gwrug	*he, she did*	**gwrussa**	*he, she would do*
gwrussyn	*we did*	**gwrussen**	*we would do*
gwrussowgh	*you* (p) *did*	**gwrussewgh**	*you* (p) *would do*
gwrussons	*they did*	**gwrussens**	*they would do*

present subjunctive		imperfect subjunctive	
gwrylliv	*I may do*	**gwrellen**	*I might do*
gwrylli	*you* (s) *may do*	**gwrelles**	*you* (s) *might do*
gwrello	*he, she may do*	**gwrella**	*he, she might do*
gwryllyn	*we may do*	**gwrellen**	*we might do*
gwryllowgh	*you* (p) *may do*	**gwrellewgh**	*you* (p) *might do*
gwrellons	*they may do*	**gwrellens**	*they might do*

Imperative

	(no 1st person singular)
gwra	*do* (s)
gwres	*let him/her do*
gwren	*let us do*
gwrewgh	*do* (p)
gwrens	*let them do*

The mutations undergone are:

State 2:	**GW**	**>**	**W**
State 4:	**GW**	**>**	**KW**
State 5:	**GW**	**>**	**HW**

The participles are:

present:	**ow kul**	*doing*
past:	**gwrys**	*done*

The main function of **gul** is to form compound tenses with other verbs. *'I see'* can be expressed as:

my a wel   or   **my a wra gweles**

The latter means *'I do see'*, and also conveys futurity by meaning *'I shall see'*. Since **gweles** and almost all other Cornish verbs have no simple future tense, this is important.

my a wra gweles Yowann hedhyw
I see John today
my a wra gweles Yowann a-vorow
I shall see John tomorrow

In compound constructions such as these, the infinitive used (in this case **gweles)** is considered as the object of **gul**. We may place this first and (as we have seen in VII 2) make the verb agree with its subject:

gweles Yowann hedhyw a wrav vy

Or we may begin with the adverb:

hedhyw y hwrav vy gweles Yowann

Questions are asked as follows:

a wre'ta gweles Yowann ?   *will you see John ?*

and negatives are used thus:

ny wrons i gweles Yowann   *they won't see John*

With the use of the auxiliary **gul**, sentences using any verb in the language (except **bos** and other auxiliaries) can be constructed, whether one knows how to conjugate the verb or not:

ev a wra poenya dhe'n gorsav   *he will run to the station*
trewa warnodho a wrons   *they spit upon him*

The preterite tense is used for a completed action in the past:

an tiek a wrug gonis y has   *the farmer sowed his seed*
gwari peldroes a wrussons   *they played football*

Questions are asked and answered by using the appropriate form of **gul**:

a wrussowgh hwi gwaynya ? *did you win ?*
  gwrussyn/na wrussyn   *yes/no*
a wrussons i dos ?   *did they come ?*
  gwrussons   *yes*

gul can also be used as a verb in its own right with the meaning *'to make'*:

ev a wrug tansys y'n lowarth
he made a bonfire in the garden

35

The imperfect tense is used for continuing action in the past:

Yowann a wre redya lyver nowydh
John was (habitually) *reading a new book*
an dus a wre kewsel yndella
folk used to speak thus

The perfect tense (see section XVIII of the Grammar) is formed by prefixing **re²**:

my re wrug redya an lyver na   *I have read that book*

When a pronoun is the object of a compound tense with **gul**, it appears as a possessive before the infinitive of the verb:

my re wrug y redya   *I have read it*
a wruss'ta aga gweles ?   *did you see them ?*

2) THE CONJUGATION AND USE OF 'MYNNES'

present tense		imperfect tense	
mynnav	*I want*	**mynnen**	*I was wanting*
mynnydh	*you* (s) *want*	**mynnes**	*you* (s) *were wanting*
mynn	*he, she wants*	**mynna**	*he, she was wanting*
mynnyn	*we want*	**mynnen**	*we were wanting*
mynnowgh	*you* (p) *want*	**mynnewgh**	*you* (p) *were wanting*
mynnons	*they want*	**mynnens**	*they were wanting*

preterite tense		conditional tense	
mynnis	*I wanted*	**mynnsen**	*I would want*
mynnsys	*you* (s) *wanted*	**mynnses**	*you* (s) *would want*
mynnas	*he, she wanted*	**mynnsa**	*he, she would want*
mynnsyn	*we wanted*	**mynnsen**	*we would want*
mynnsowgh	*you* (p) *wanted*	**mynnsewgh**	*you* (p) *would want*
mynnsons	*they wanted*	**mynnsens**	*they would want*

present subjunctive		imperfect subjunctive	
mynniv	*I may want*	**mynnen**	*I might want*
mynni	*you* (s) *may want*	**mynnes**	*you* (s) *might want*
mynno	*he, she may want*	**mynna**	*he, she might want*
mynnyn	*we may want*	**mynnen**	*we might want*
mynnowgh	*you* (p) *may want*	**mynnewgh**	*you* (p) *might want*
mynnons	*they may want*	**mynnens**	*they might want*

The mutations undergone by **mynnes** are:

State 2: **M > V**
State 5: **M > F**

When used as an auxiliary **mynnes** conveys willingness or intention.

my a wra mos	*I shall go* (statement of fact)
my a vynn mos	*I want to go* (intention)

Here are some more examples of the use of **mynnes**, which are self-explanatory in the light of what has gone before:

a vynnsys ta y weles ?	*did you want to see him ?*
mynnis/na vynnis	*yes/no*
distowgh y fynnav mos tre	*I want to go home forthwith*
ny vynnav vy mos	*I don't want to go*

Note that **mynnes** must always have a verb predicate and not a noun. It would be quite wrong to say:

*a vynnowgh hwi hanafas a de ?
do you want a cup of tea ?

A main verb must be included:

a vynnowgh hwi kavoes hanafas a de ?
do you want (to have) a cup of tea ?

However, when a noun immediately follows in the predicate, **orth** must be inserted:

my a vynn orth Yowann dybri y vara
I want John to eat his bread

present tense		imperfect tense	
gallav	*I can*	**gyllyn**	*I was able*
gyllydh	*you* (s) *can*	**gyllys**	*you* (s) *were able*
gyll	*he, she can*	**gylli**	*he, she was able*
gyllyn	*we can*	**gyllyn**	*we were able*
gyllowgh	*you* (p) *can*	**gyllewgh**	*you* (p) *were able*
gyllons	*they can*	**gyllens**	*they were able*

preterite tense		conditional tense	
gyllis	*I could*	**gallsen**	*I would be able*
gyllsys	*you* (s) *could*	**gallses**	*you* (s) *would be able*
gallas	*he, she could*	**gallsa**	*he, she would be able*
gyllsyn	*we* (p) *could*	**gallsen**	*we would be able*
gyllsowgh	*you could*	**gallsewgh**	*you* (p) *would be able*
gallsons	*they could*	**gallsens**	*they would be able*

present subjunctive		imperfect subjunctive	
gylliv	*I may be able*	**gallen**	*I might be able*
gylli	*you may be able*	**galles**	*you* (s) *might be able*
gallo	*he, she may be able*	**galla**	*he, she might be able*
gyllyn	*we may be able*	**gallen**	*we might be able*
gyllowgh	*you may be able*	**gallewgh**	*you* (p) *might be able*
gallons	*they may be able*	**gallens**	*they might be able*

The mutations undergone by **galloes** are:

State 2:	**G** disappears
State 4:	**G > K**
State 5:	**G > H**

The use of **galloes** is quite straightforward; it simply translates the English *'can'* or *'be able'* in all its tenses, provided that the ability concerned is physical rather than mental:

my a yll gweles an mor	*I can see the sea*
gweles an mor a allav vy	
a yllowgh hwi dos ?	*can you come ?*
gyllyn/na yllyn	*yes/no*

warlyna y hylli ev	*last year he used to be able*
gwari peldroes	*to play football*
ny yllons i redya	*they cannot read*

Note that in the last two examples, physical impossibility is implied, not lack of skill. In the case of mental ability, **godhvos** is used. Compare the following:

hi a yll kana	*she can sing*
	(her vocal chords function)
hi a woer kana	*she can sing* (she has been trained to)

The present tense will express a present or future time depending on the context:

a yllons i dos hedhyw ?	*can they come today ?*
a yllons i dos a-vorow ?	*can they come tomorrow ?*

APPENDIX 1: MUTATIONS AND THEIR CAUSES

<u>State 2:</u> (soft mutation) **P > B**   **T > D**   **K > G**
                          B > V   **D > DH** **G > W** or lost
                          M > V   **CH > J**

*   an *'the'* mutates feminine singular nouns and masculine plurals of persons (but not things);
*   the above nouns mutate the first following adjective;
*   preceding adjectives, such as **hen** *'old'* and **tebel** *'evil'*, mutate their nouns;
*   the following particles mutate the verb: **a, ny, na, re** (except for before parts of **bos**), **yn unn, om-**;
*   the possessives **dha** *'your'* (s) and **y** *'his'* mutate their nouns;
*   the numeral **unn** *'one'* mutates a feminine noun;
*   the numerals **dew** and **diw** *'two'* mutate their nouns and are themselves 95mutated by **an**;
*   the following words mutate whatever follows:

mar	*so*	**a**	*of*	**pan**	*when*	**dell**	*as*
pur	*very*	**war**	*on*	**erna**	*until*	**fatell**	*how*
re	*too*	**dhe**	*to*	**kettell**	*as soon as*	**dre**	*through*

*   **heb** 'without' mutates only in a few conventional phrases such as **heb wow** 'without a lie/really/is that so?'.

<u>State 3:</u> (aspirate mutation)   **P > F**   **T > TH**   **K > H**

*   the possessives **ow** *'my'*, **hy** *'her'* and **aga** *'their'*;
*   the numerals **tri** and **teyr** *'three'*.

<u>State 4:</u> (hard mutation)   **B > P**   **D > T**   **G > K**

*   the verbal particle **ow**, forming the present participle;
*   **mar** *'if'* and **a** *'if'*;

<u>State 5:</u> (mixed mutation)   **B > F**   **D > T**   **G > H**
                                     M > F

*   the verbal particle **y**;
*   **yn**, which forms adverbs from adjectives;
*   suffixed possessive **'th** *'your'* (s);
*   object pronoun **'th** *'you'* (s);
*   words where the **y** particle is integral or implied:

may	*so that*	**kyn**	*although*
ple	*where*	**p'eur**	*when*

APPENDIX 2   FORMATION OF NOUNS, ADJECTIVES

1)   Many nouns can be formed from adjectives by suffixing **-der** or **-ter**:

toemm	*warm*	**toemmder**	*warmth*
yeyn	*cold*	**yeynder**	*coldness*
teg	*beautiful*	**tekter**	*beauty*
da	*good*	**dader**	*goodness*
drog	*bad*	**drokter**	*evil*

All such nouns are masculine in gender.

2)   A useful suffix is **-va**, which signifies *'a place where something happens'*:

soedh	*work*	**soedhva**	*office*
lyver	*book*	**lyverva**	*library*
lyther	*letter*	**lytherva**	*post-office*

All such nouns are feminine in gender.

3)   The prefix **kes-** signifies *'co-'*

kows	*speech*	**keskows**	*conversation*

an Kenedhlow Kesunys   *the United Nations*

4)   The prefixes **di-**, **dis-** signify *'without'*:

bro	*country*	**divro**	*stateless*
kommol	*clouds*	**digommol**	*cloudless*
gwrys	*done*	**diswrys**	*undone*

Note the State 2 mutation caused.

5)   Verbs can be formed from adjectives by suffixing **-he**:

glan	*clean*	**glanhe**	*to clean*
gwell	*better*	**gwellhe**	*to improve*
toemm	*warm*	**toemmhe**	*to warm*

All such verbs are fairly regular (past participle in **-hes**).

6)   The ending **-ek** is the commonest adjectival suffix:

reden	*ferns*	**redenek**	*ferny (place)*

It often signifies *'an abundance'*. One of the Bards of the Gorsedh had very bushy eyebrows **(abrans)**, and his bardic name was **Abransek** *'very eyebrowy'*.

7)   The ending **-us** (pronounced [-Is], being unstressed), is also adjectival and signifies *'giving rise to a quality'*:

hwarth	*laugh*	**hwarthus**	*laughable*
pita	*pity*	**pitedhus**	*pitiable*
skwith	*tired*	**skwithus**	*fatiguing*

Other publications from *Kesva an Taves Kernewe*k
(The Cornish Language Board) include:

Grammar Beyond the First Grade by **John Page**
ISBN 0 907064 14 0, 48 pages, softbound
a follow up to this present volume

An Gerlyver Kres (The New Standard Cornish Dictionary)
by **Dr Ken George**
ISBN 0 907064 79 5, 320 pages, hardback
The Cornish-English, English-Cornish Dictionary

A Grammar of Modern Cornish by **Wella Brown**
ISBN 1 902917 00 6, 321 pages, hardback
a comprehensive and detailed description
of Cornwall's own language - for the advanced student

Cornish This Way ~ Holyewgh an Lergh
by **Graham Sandercock** ISBN 0 907064 95 7, 64 A4 pages, softback, *a*
course for beginners in Cornish plus accompanying double cassette
ISBN 0 907064 17 5, three hours running time

The First Thousand Words in Cornish ISBN 1 902917 25 1
the Cornish version of this popular and colourful series for children
and adults alike (to be republished 2002)

THESE TITLES, AND MORE, AND DETAILS OF CORNISH
COURSES ARE AVAILABLE FROM:

GEORGE ANSELL,
CORNISH LANGUAGE BOARD PUBLICATIONS,
65 Churchtown,
Gwinear,
Hayle,
Cornwall
Tel and Fax: 01736 850878